THIS AWESOME

SKETCHBOOK

BELONGS TO

DATE

DATE ______________

DATE ____________

DATE

DATE

DATE

DATE

DATE ____________

DATE

DATE

DATE ______________

DATE

DATE

DATE

DATE

DATE

DATE

DATE

DATE

DATE ____________

DATE ____________

DATE

DATE

DATE

DATE

DATE ____________

DATE ______________

DATE

DATE

DATE

DATE

DATE

DATE

DATE

DATE

DATE

DATE

DATE

DATE ____________

DATE

DATE

DATE

DATE

DATE ______________

DATE ______________

DATE

DATE

DATE ______________

DATE ____________

DATE

DATE ____________

DATE

DATE ______________

DATE

DATE

DATE ____________

DATE

DATE

DATE

DATE

DATE ______________

DATE ______________

DATE

DATE ______________

DATE ____________

DATE ____________

DATE ____________

DATE ____________

DATE

DATE

DATE

DATE

DATE ______________

DATE ______________

DATE

DATE

DATE

DATE

DATE

DATE

DATE

DATE ____________

DATE

DATE

DATE

DATE

DATE

DATE ______________

DATE

DATE ______________

DATE

DATE

DATE

DATE

DATE

DATE ______________

DATE ______________

DATE ____________

DATE

DATE

DATE ______________

DATE ______________

DATE ____________

DATE ____________

DATE

DATE

DATE

DATE ______________

www.ingramcontent.com/pod-product-compliance
Lightning Source LLC
Chambersburg PA
CBHW081006170526
45158CB00010B/2931
9781091103405